AF269969

Managing Editor
Ina Massler Levin, M.A.

Editor
Eric Migliaccio

Contributing Editor
Sarah Smith

Creative Director
Karen J. Goldfluss, M.S. Ed.

Cover Design
Tony Carrillo / Marilyn Goldberg

Teacher Created Resources

12621 Western Avenue
Garden Grove, CA 92841
www.teachercreated.com

ISBN: 978-1-4206-5958-0

©2007 Teacher Created Resources
Reprinted, 2023 (PO604802)
Made in U.S.A.

The material in this book is intended for individual use only. No part of this publication may be transmitted, reproduced, stored, or recorded in any form without written permission from the publisher.

This book belongs to

____

Ready·Set·Learn

Get Ready to Learn!

Get ready, get set, and go! Boost your child's learning with this exciting series of books. Geared to help children practice and master many needed skills, the *Ready·Set·Learn* books are bursting with 64 pages of learning fun. Use these books for . . .

 enrichment    skills reinforcement    extra practice

With their smaller size, the *Ready·Set·Learn* books fit easily in children's hands, backpacks, and book bags. All your child needs to get started are pencils, crayons, and colored pencils.

A full sheet of colorful stickers is included. Use these stickers for . . .

- decorating pages

- rewarding outstanding effort

- keeping track of completed pages

Celebrate your child's progress by using these stickers on the reward chart located on the inside cover. The blue-ribbon sticker fits perfectly on the certificate on page 64.

With *Ready·Set·Learn* and a little encouragement, your child will be on the fast track to learning fun!

Uppercase Letters

Directions: Copy each uppercase letter.

A   B   C   D

E   F   G   H

I   J   K   L

M   N   O   P

Q   R   S   T

U   V   W   X

Y   Z

Lowercase Letters

Directions: Copy each lowercase letter.

a   b   c   d

e   f   g   h

i   j   k   l

m   n   o   p

q   r   s   t

u   v   w   x

y   z

Short "Aa" Words

Directions: Blend the letter sounds together as you say each word. Then color the picture it names.

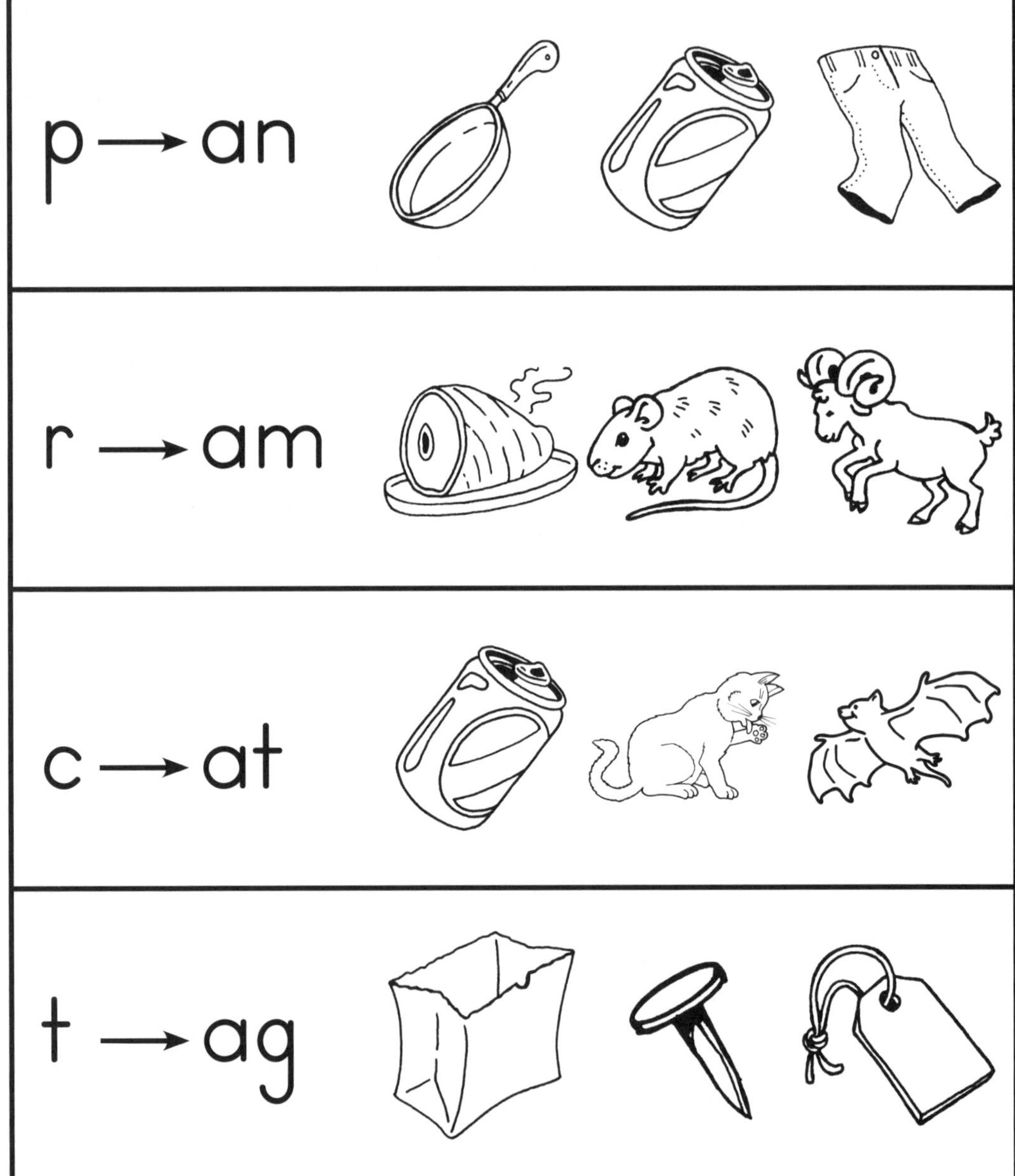

Short "Ee" Words

Directions: Finish each word with "et" or "en." Color the pictures.

Directions: Finish each word with "est" or "ell." Color the pictures.

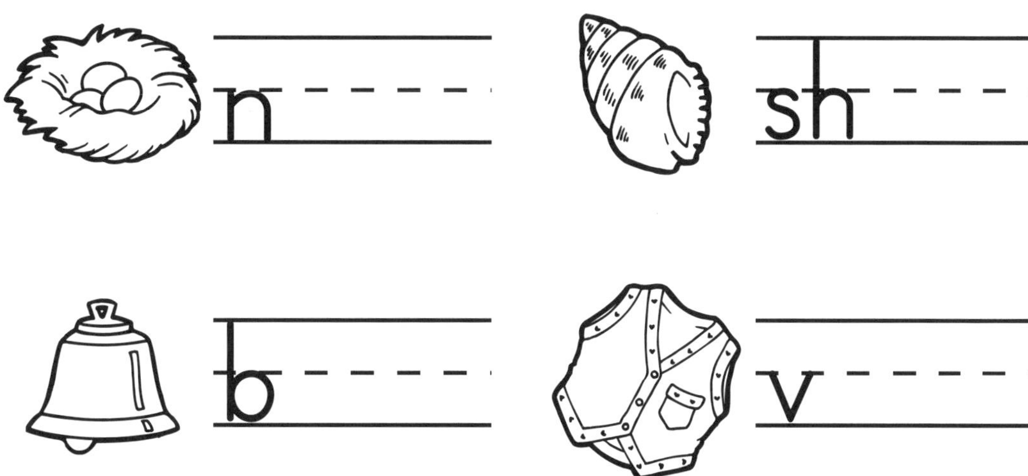

Short "Ii" Words

Directions: Unscramble the words. Write them on the lines.

lip	mill	sit
hit	grin	pill

©Teacher Created Resources, Inc.

Short "Oo" Words

Directions: Write the name of each picture below. Then, circle the letter that represents the short *o* sound.

1.	**5.**
__________	__________
2.	**6.**
__________	__________
3.	**7.**
__________	__________
4.	**8.**
__________	__________

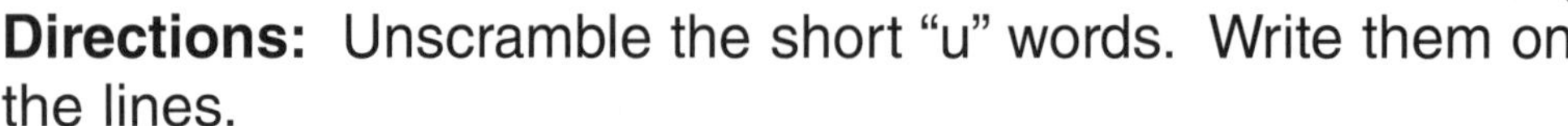

Short "Uu" Words

Directions: Unscramble the short "u" words. Write them on the lines.

ppu _______________   uppm _______________

umpj _______________   pu _______________

pcu _______________   mupl _______________

Long "Aa" Words

Directions: Fill in missing letters under the pictures. Then write the words in the correct word family below each picture.

day	date	hay
make	bake	lake
say	gate	late

_____ay   _____ake   _____ate

Long "Ee" Words

Directions: Finish each word with "ee" or "ea."

w___d

f___t

h___t

k___p

n___d

wh___t

sh___p

m___t

n___t

f___d

bl___d

sp___d

Long "Ii" Words

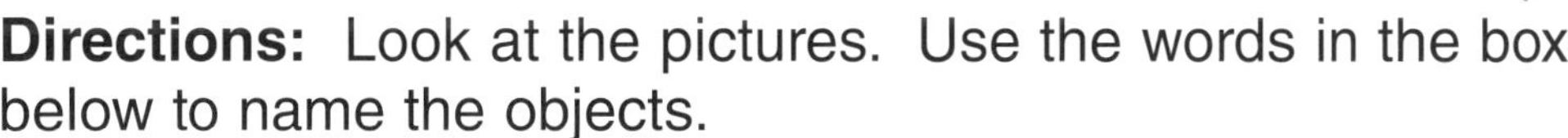

Directions: Look at the pictures. Use the words in the box below to name the objects.

1.

4.

2.

5.

3.

6.

dice	ice	pine
night	mice	vine

Long "Oo" Words

Directions: Finish each word with "old" or "oat."

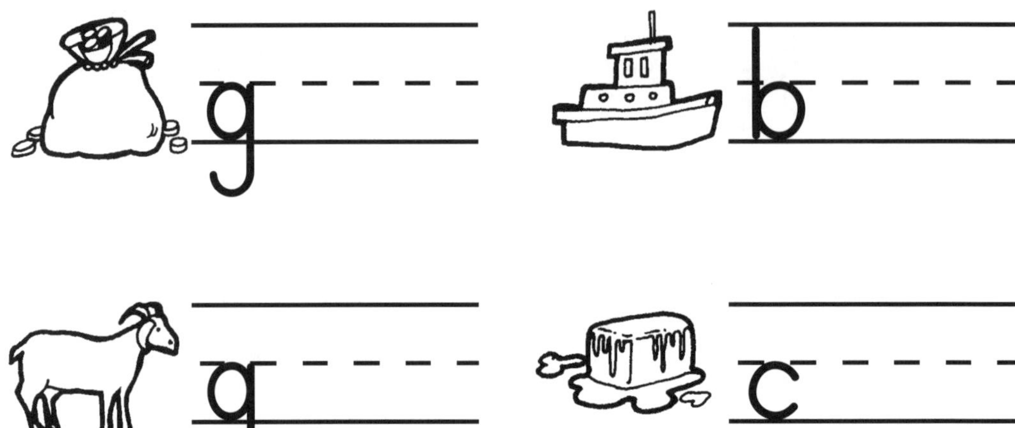

Directions: Finish each word with "oke" or "ow."

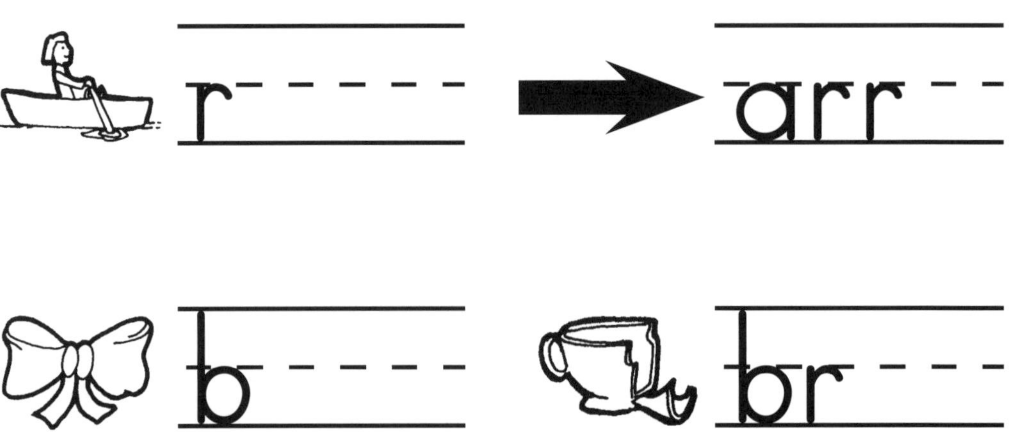

Long "Uu" Words

Directions: Unscramble the words. Write the long "u" words on the lines.

cube	huge	tube
dune	mule	tune

gueh _______________

lume _______________

ebtu _______________

dneu _______________

becu _______________

eutn _______________

Missing Vowels

Directions: Say the picture names. Write the missing vowels.

<table>
<tr><td>

1.

b __ t

</td><td>

4.

r ___ ck

</td></tr>
<tr><td>

2.

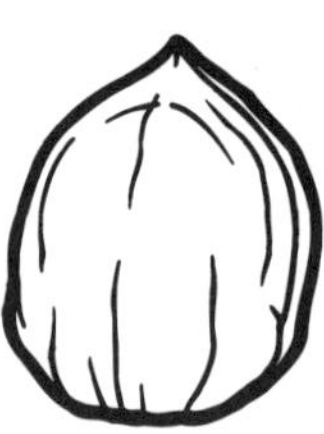

n __ t

</td><td>

5.

b ___ x

</td></tr>
<tr><td>

3.

m __ c __

</td><td>

6.

t r ___ ___ n

</td></tr>
</table>

16

©Teacher Created Resources, Inc.

"Bl" and "Br" Blends

Directions: Color the pictures that begin either with the "bl" or "br" sound.

Many Blends

Directions: Say the name for each picture. On the line, write the blend you hear at the beginning of the word.

Listen for the **r** blends as in **trap** and **grass.**

Listen for the **l** blends as in **flag** and **slide.**

Listen for the **s** blends as in **smile** and **swim.**

Ending Blends

Directions: Say the name for each picture. Find the word that names the picture. Write it beside the picture. Underline the ending blend.

skunk   **desk**   **ring**   **plant**   **jump**

1.

2.

3.

4.

5.

Words in a Family

Directions: Say the name for each picture. Write the beginning sound. Then, read all the words in each word family out loud.

1. **an**	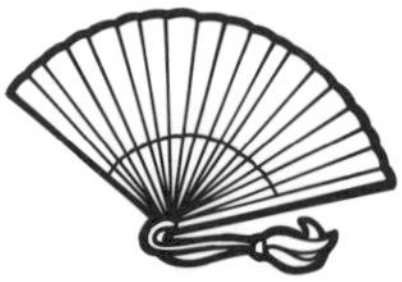 _____ an	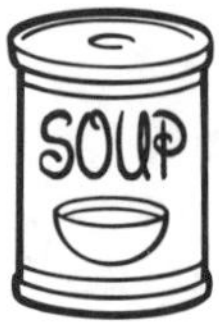 _____ an	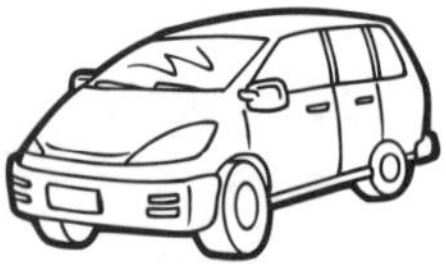 _____ an
2. **et**	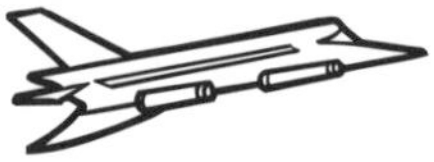 _____ et	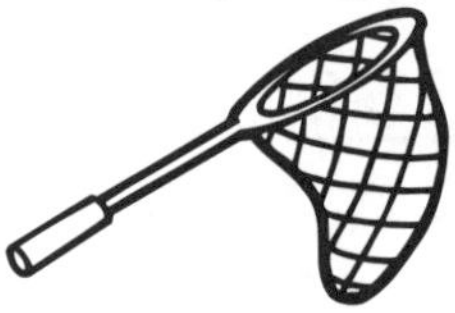 _____ et	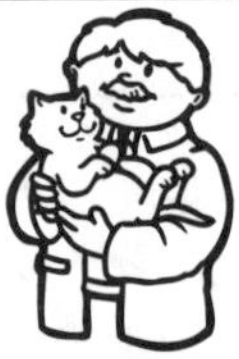 _____ et
3. **and**	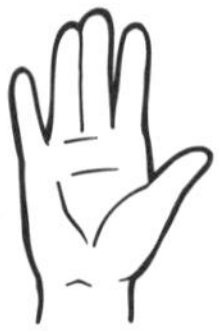 _____ and	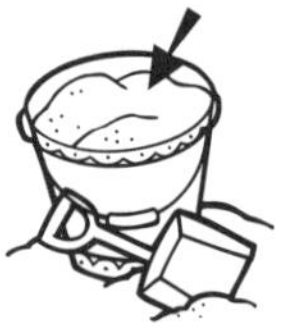 _____ and	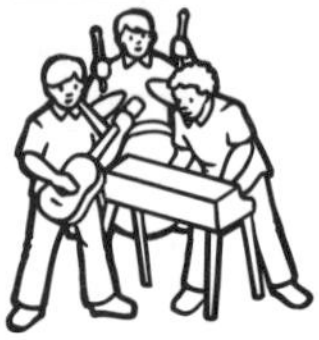 _____ and
4. **op**	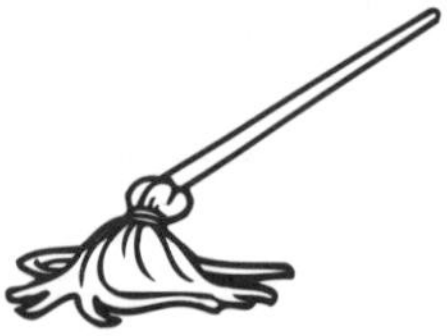 _____ op	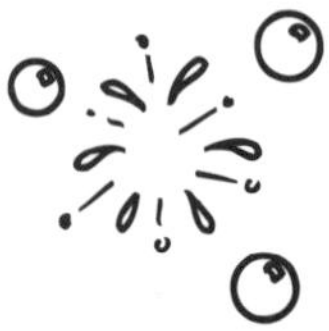 _____ op	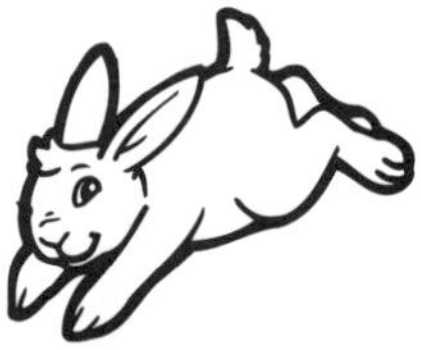 _____ op

Short or Long?

Directions: Say the name for each picture. On the line, print the vowel sound that you hear. If the vowel is **short**, fill in the bubble labeled **short**. If the vowel is **long**, fill in the bubble labeled **long**.

1.  ○ short ○ long	**2.**  ○ short ○ long	**3.**  ○ short ○ long
4.  ○ short ○ long	**5.**  ○ short ○ long	**6.**  ○ short ○ long
7.  ○ short ○ long	**8.**  ○ short ○ long	**9.**  ○ short ○ long

Which Short Vowel?

Directions: Read each sentence. Circle the word that best completes the sentence and write it on the line.

	1. The dog sat in the _______________ .	set sun sick
	2. The pig is on the _______________ .	mop map mat
	3. The bug is in the _______________ .	top net nest
	4. I put him in the _______________ .	tub tan top
	5. He can _______________ .	dig den dot
	6. A fish has a _______________ .	fat fin fell

Two Meanings

Directions: Look at each pair of pictures. Write a word that names both pictures. Use the words from the Word Bank to help you.

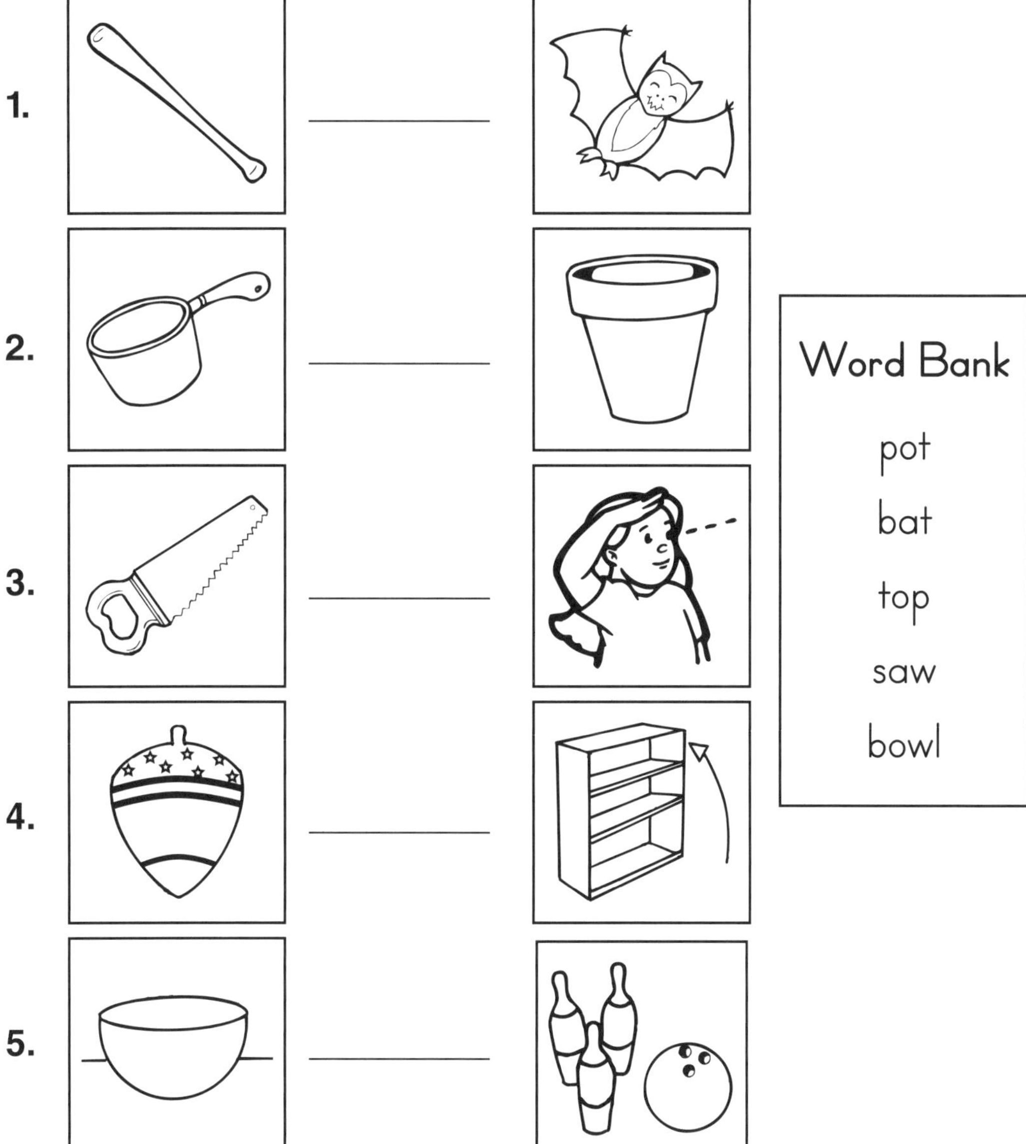

Rhyming Sentences

Directions: Complete the blank in each sentence with a word that rhymes with the underlined word. Use the words from the Rhyming Word Bank to help you.

Rhyming Word Bank		
truck	hat	fish
box	book	frog

1. 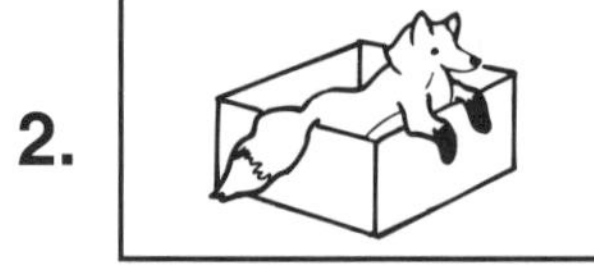 Look at the _____________________.

2.  The fox is in a _____________________.

3.  On the log sits a _____________________.

4.  The cat wears a _____________________.

5.  There is a duck in my _____________________.

6. I wish I had a _____________________.

Myrtle Turtle's Sight Words

Directions: Myrtle is a sight word turtle. She had to hide in her shell in a hurry. She scrambled her sight words. What a mess! Write the sight words correctly on her shell.

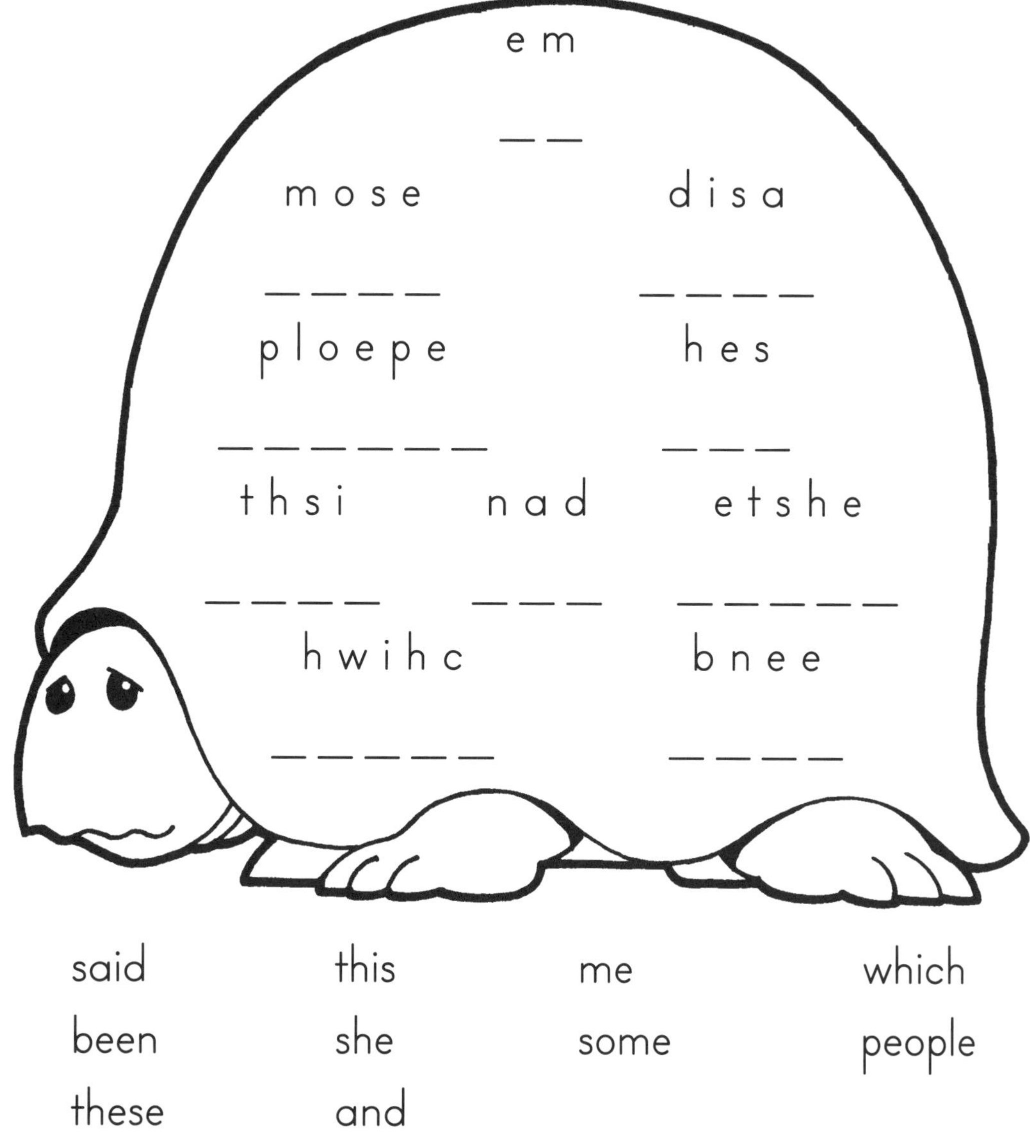

said   this   me   which

been   she   some   people

these   and

Animal ABC Order

Directions: Put these words in alphabetical order.

1.

____

____

____

____

2.

____

____

____

____

3.

____

____

____

____

4.

____

____

____

____

Same Letter ABC Order

Directions: Put these words in alphabetical order.

<table>
<tr><td>

1.

doll __________

dance __________

drive __________

dinosaur __________

deer __________

</td><td>

2.

gum __________

gate __________

glue __________

goat __________

grape __________

</td></tr>
<tr><td>

3.

melt __________

monkey __________

milk __________

math __________

mud __________

</td><td>

4.

snake __________

sail __________

slide __________

soft __________

smell __________

</td></tr>
</table>

Controlled Rr Words

Directions: Say the name for each picture. Print its name under it. Use the list of words to help you.

tractor	turkey	corn
bird	shark	yarn

1.

2.

3.

4.

5.

6.

28

©Teacher Created Resources, Inc.

Identifying Digraphs

Directions: Read the word in the first column. Write the digraph in the second column. Fill in the bubble in the third column to show if the digraph is heard at the beginning, in the middle, or at the end of the word.

Digraphs			
ch	sh	th	wh

Word	Digraph	Position in Word Beginning Middle End
1. cherry	ch	● ○ ○
2. match		○ ○ ○
3. father		○ ○ ○
4. mouth		○ ○ ○
5. wash		○ ○ ○
6. lunch		○ ○ ○
7. sheep		○ ○ ○
8. teacher		○ ○ ○
9. whale		○ ○ ○

Describe It

Directions: Write a word that describes each picture below.
Use the words in the Word Bank to help you.

<table>
<tr><td colspan="3" align="center">Word Bank</td></tr>
<tr><td>hot</td><td>three</td><td>smelly</td></tr>
<tr><td>quiet</td><td>cute</td><td>big</td></tr>
</table>

1. 

____

- - - - - - - - -

____

2. 

____

- - - - - - - - -

____

3. 

____

- - - - - - - - -

____

4. 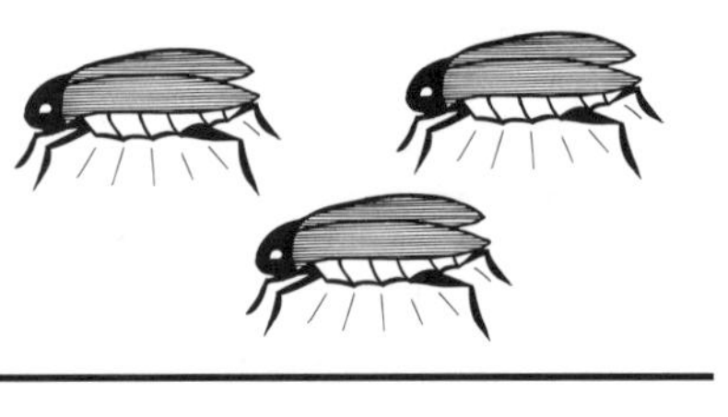

____

- - - - - - - - -

____

5. 

____

- - - - - - - - -

____

6.

____

- - - - - - - - -

____

More Than One

Directions: Write a singular noun for the first picture. Make the noun plural to match the second picture.

	Singular		Plural
Example:	ant		ants
1.			
2.			
3.			
4.			
5.			
6.			

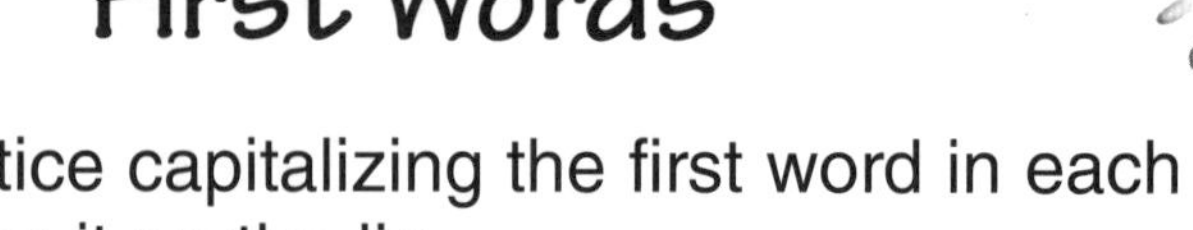

First Words

Directions: Practice capitalizing the first word in each sentence by writing it on the line.

1. _______ mom took me shopping.

   my

2. _______ we play now?

   can

3. _______ like to eat cookies.

   i

4. _______ are going to the movies.

   we

5. _______ helped me bake a cake.

   she

6. _______ are eggs in the nest.

   there

7. _______ you coming with us?

   are

End It Right

Directions: Read each sentence below. Write the correct punctuation mark at the end of the sentence.

1. Does your class have a pet

2. My class has a pet lizard

3. His name is Tiny Tim

4. One day the lizard escaped

5. We looked all over the classroom for him

6. Do you know how hard it is to find something so small

7. We looked and looked

8. Then Sandy yelled, "There he is "

9. We put him back in his cage

10. We were so happy

Connect the Dots

Directions: Count by connecting the dots in number order from 1–50.

©Teacher Created Resources, Inc.

Connect the Dots

Directions: Count by connecting the dots in number order from 50–100.

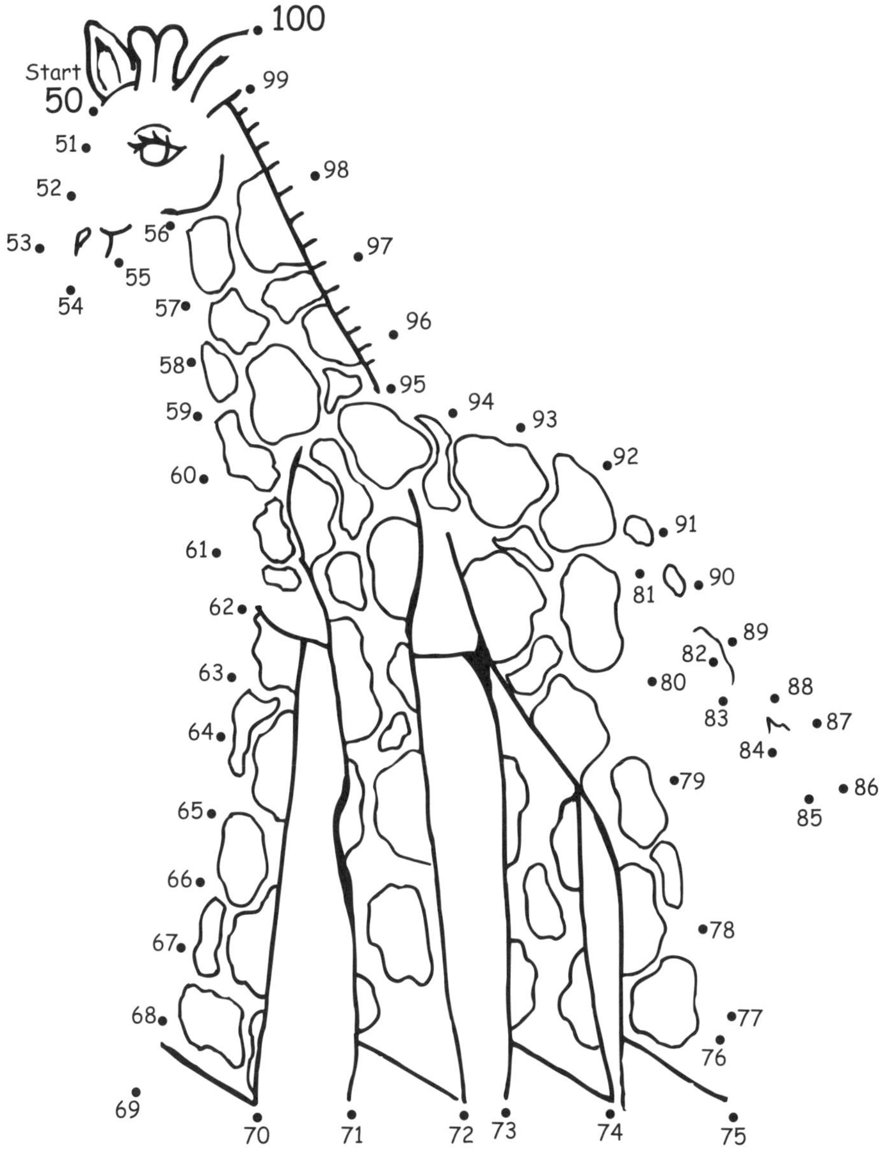

Count, Write, Name

Directions: Count the number of pictures. Write the number name. Use the Word Bank to help you.

Word Bank				
one	two	three	four	five
six	seven	eight	nine	ten

1.

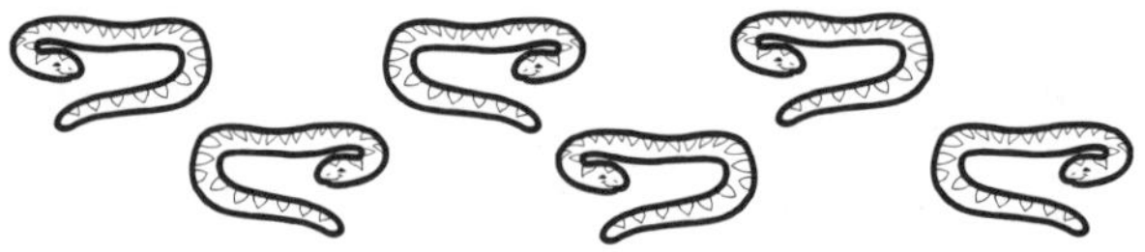

2.

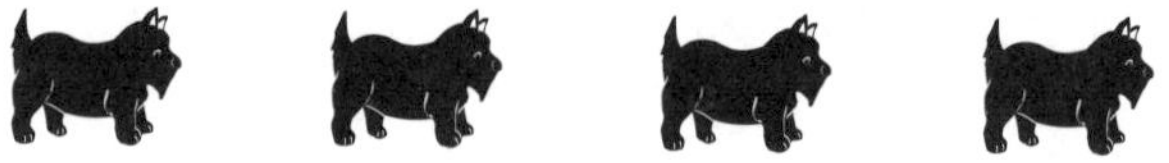

3.

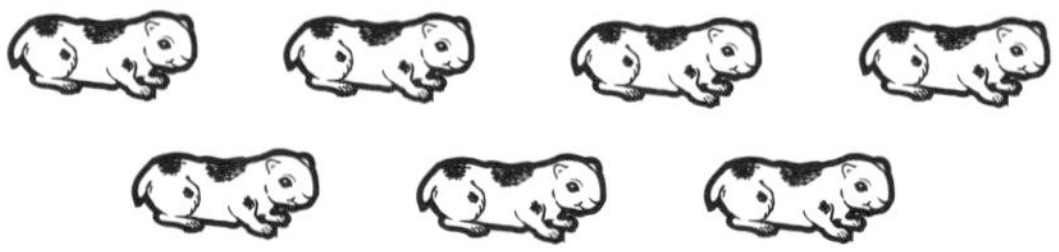

4.

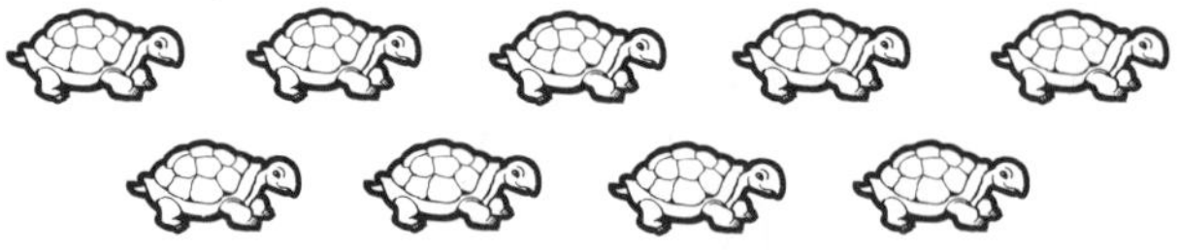

5.

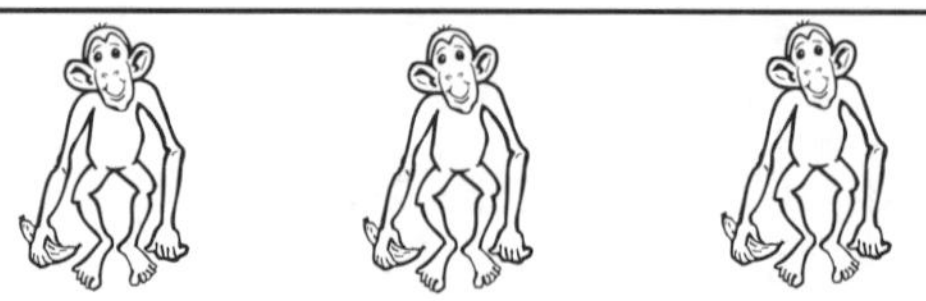

Pizza, Pizza

Directions: Count the dots. Color the puzzle.

1 = red	2 = brown	3 = yellow	4 = blue

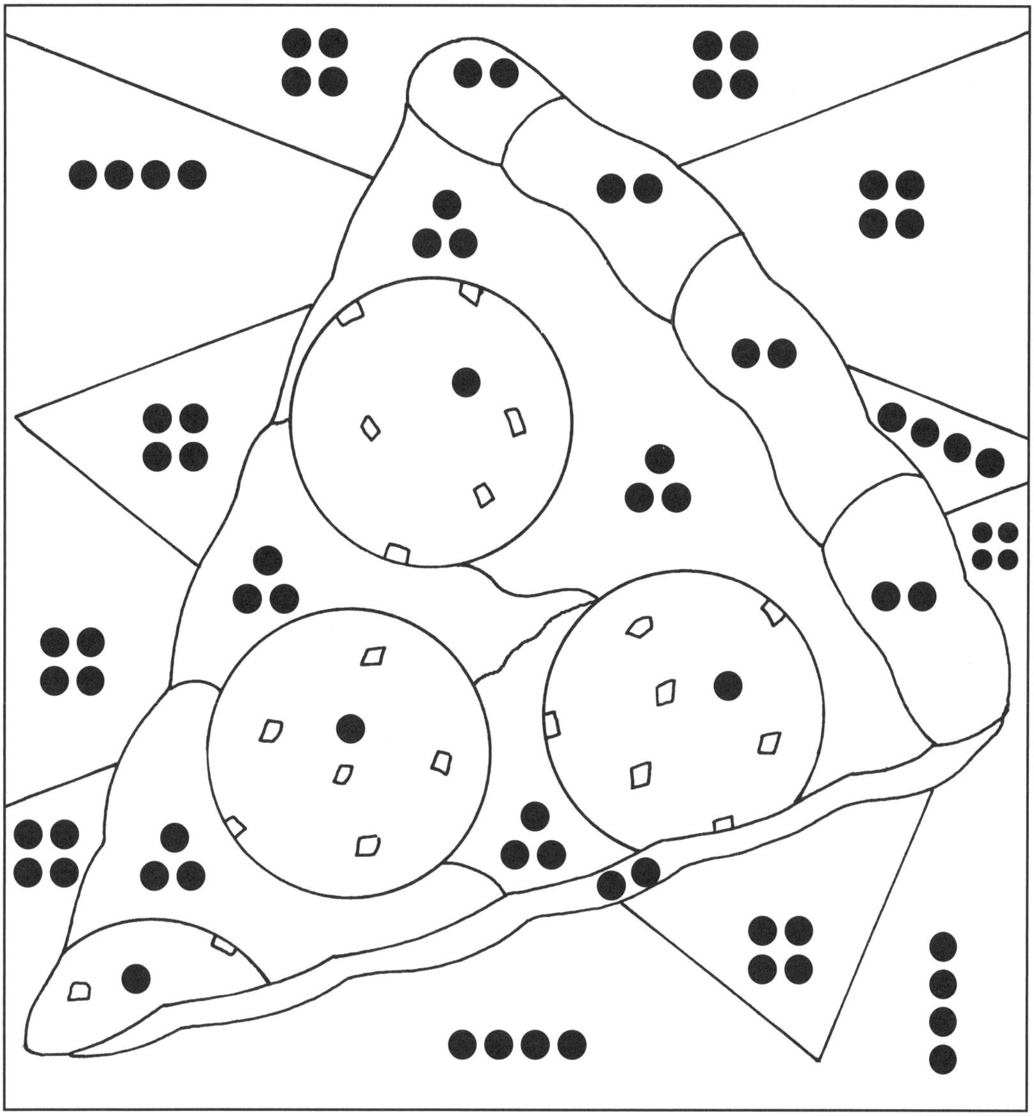

Coloring Fun

Color 3 stars yellow. 

Color 2 balls red. 

Color 1 bell blue. 

Color 3 tops yellow. 

Color 4 apples red. 

Color 5 hats blue. 

1. How many things are yellow? _______________________

2. How many things are red? _______________________

3. How many things are blue? _______________________

Everything Counts

Directions: Count and write the number of space things in the picture. Then color the pictures.

Counting by 2s

Directions: Color the numbers you say when counting by **2s**.

1	2	3	4	5	6	7	8	9	10
11	12	13	14	15	16	17	18	19	20
21	22	23	24	25	26	27	28	29	30
31	32	33	34	35	36	37	38	39	40
41	42	43	44	45	46	47	48	49	50
51	52	53	54	55	56	57	58	59	60
61	62	63	64	65	66	67	68	69	70
71	72	73	74	75	76	77	78	79	80
81	82	83	84	85	86	87	88	89	90
91	92	93	94	95	96	97	98	99	100

Counting by 5s

Directions: Help Max get home by counting by 5s.

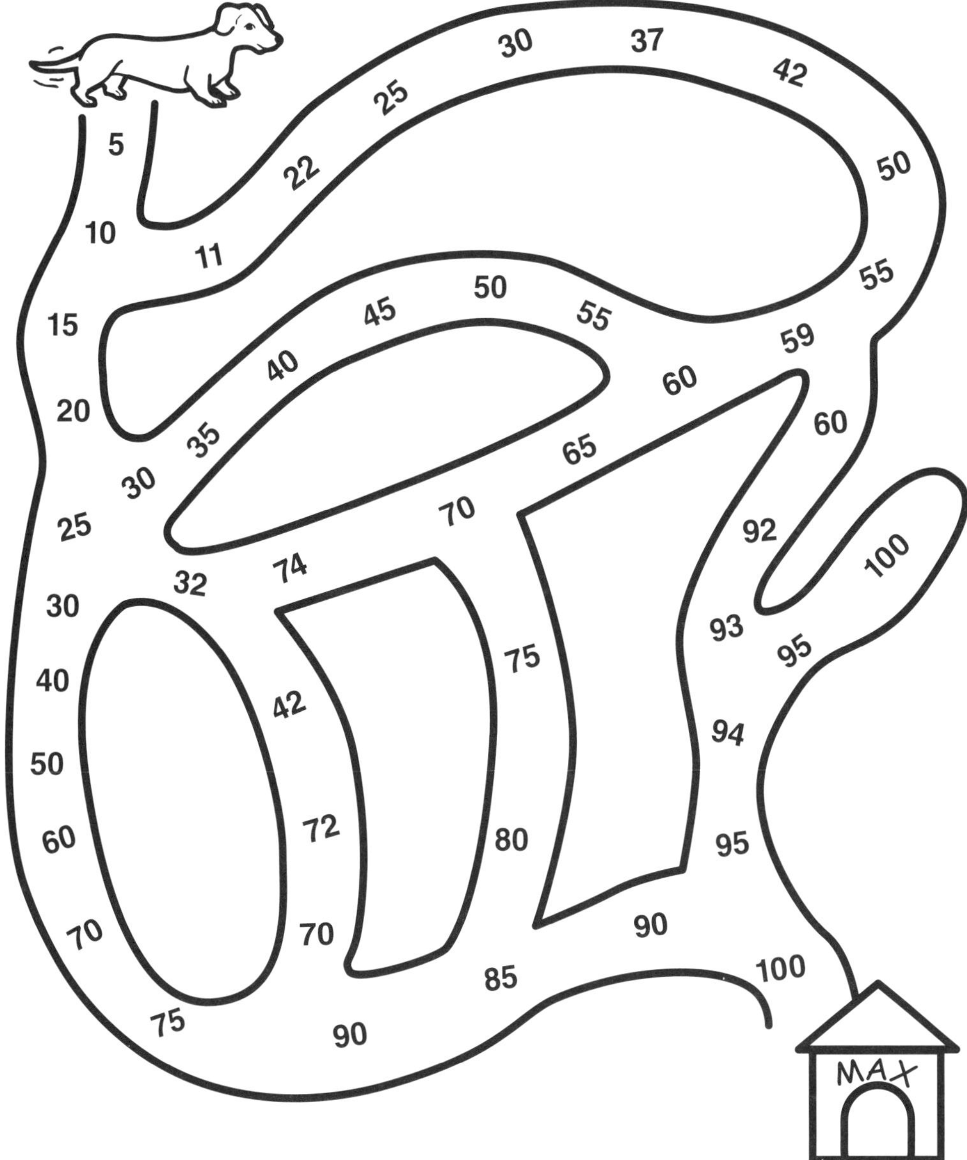

Counting by 10s

Directions: Count by **10s** to complete the dot-to-dot.

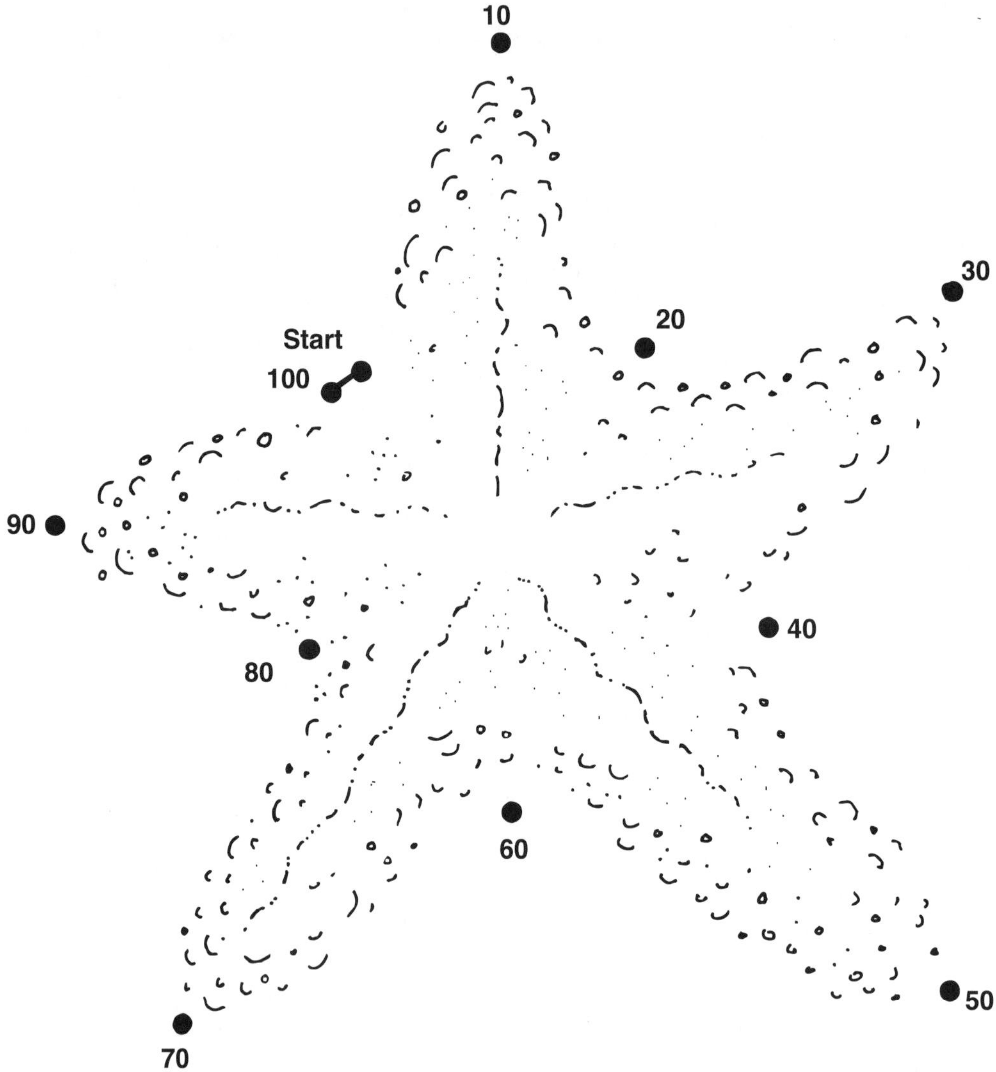

Before, After, Between

Directions: Write the number that comes before.

1. _________ 16
2. _________ 29
3. _________ 67

4. _________ 35
5. _________ 72
6. _________ 53

Directions: Write the number that comes after.

7. 19 _________
8. 93 _________
9. 62 _________

10. 38 _________
11. 84 _________
12. 55 _________

Directions: Write the number that comes between.

13. 23 _____ 25
14. 56 _____ 58
15. 94 _____ 96

16. 41 _____ 43
17. 75 _____ 77
18. 87 _____ 89

Sequencing Numbers

Directions: Place the numbers on the berries in order from least to greatest.

1.

______ ______ ______ ______ ______

2.

______ ______ ______ ______ ______

3.

______ ______ ______ ______ ______

4.

______ ______ ______ ______ ______

Odd and Even

Directions: Decide which numbers are odd and even.
Color the puzzle.

odd = red	even = blue

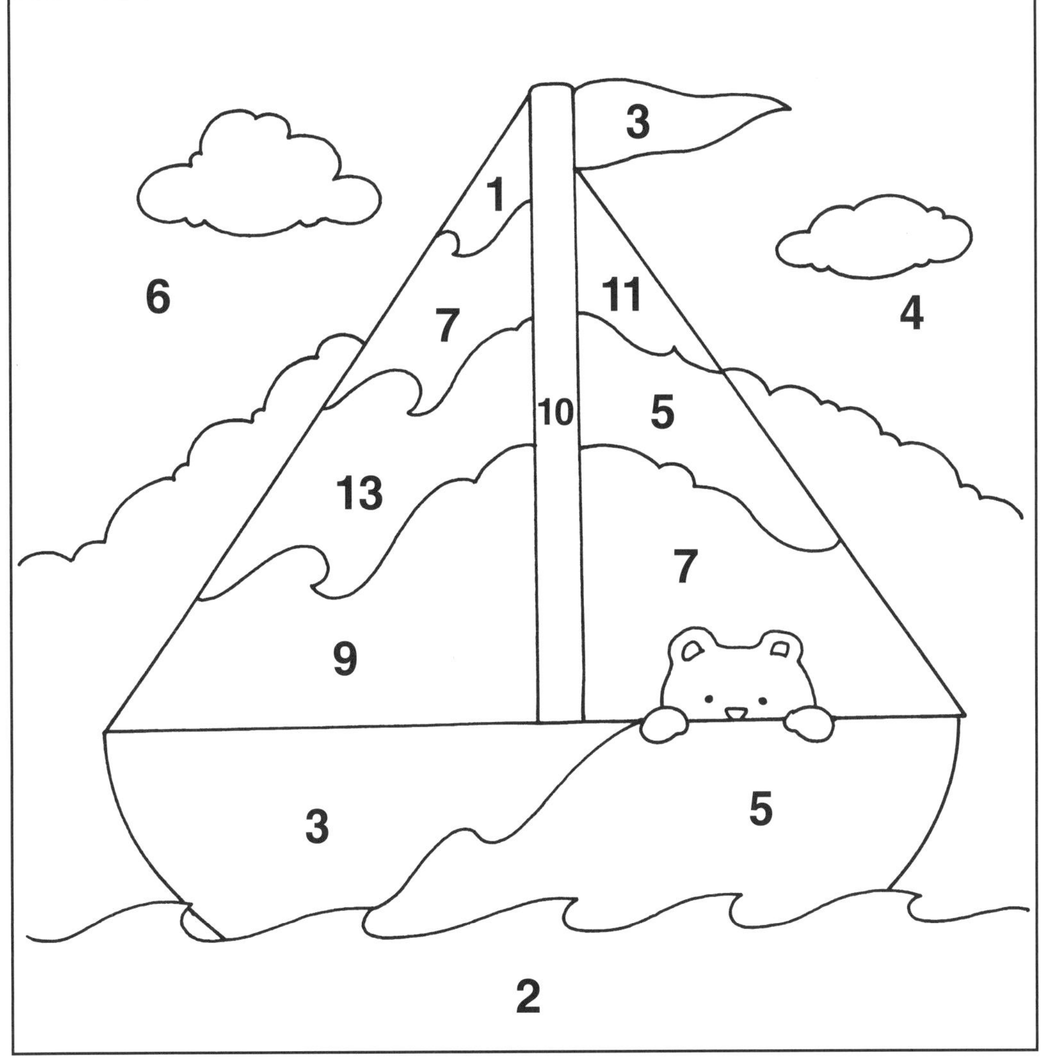

Show Addition

Directions: Write a number sentence to go with each picture.

1.
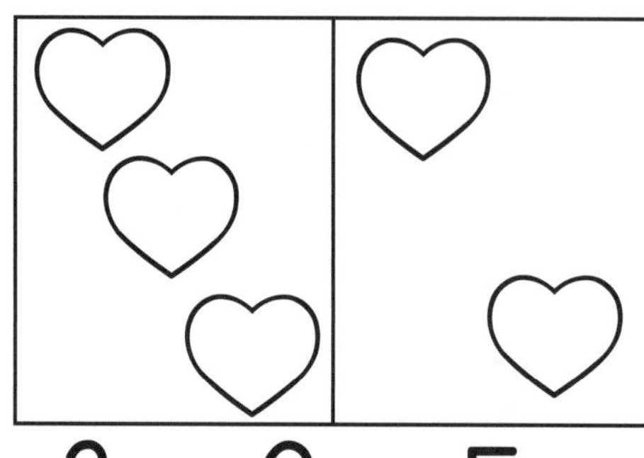

$$\underline{3} + \underline{2} = \underline{5}$$

4.
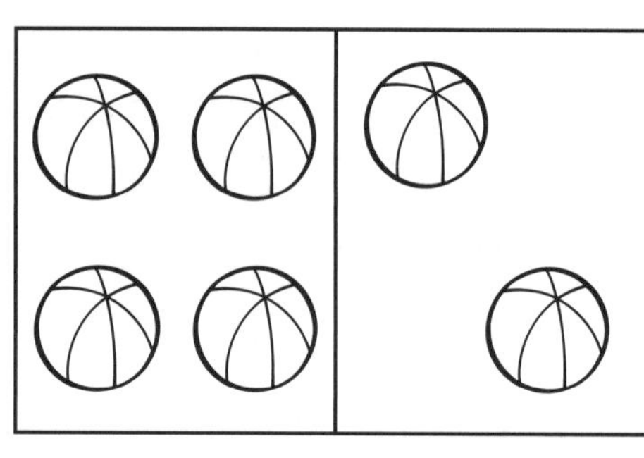

___ + ___ = ___

2.
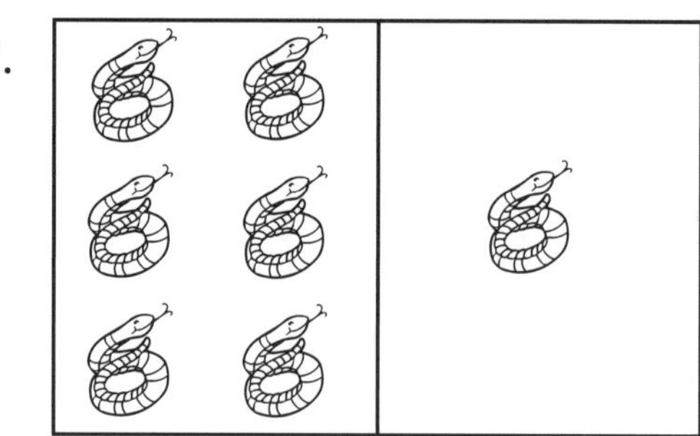

___ + ___ = ___

5.

___ + ___ = ___

3.
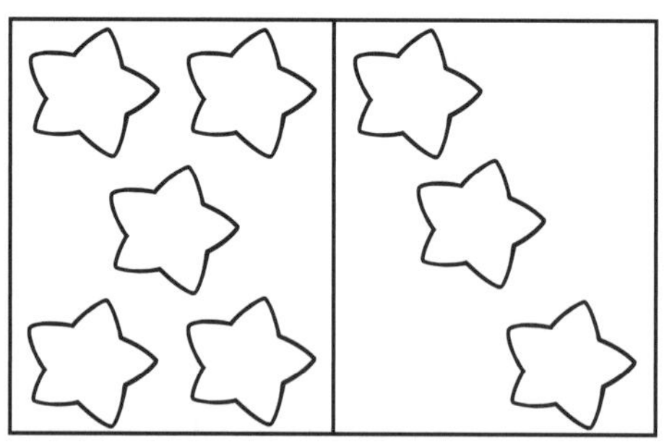

___ + ___ = ___

6.
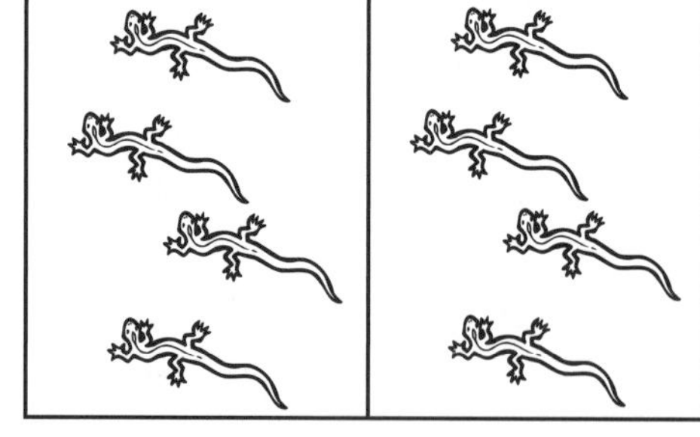

___ + ___ = ___

Books of Nine

Directions: Find the total on each book. Color each book that equals 9.

1.
$$5 + 4$$

2.
$$6 + 3$$

3.
$$2 + 2$$

4.
$$4 + 5$$

5.
$$5 + 2$$

6.
$$2 + 7$$

7.
$$1 + 8$$

8.
$$1 + 4$$

9.
$$0 + 9$$

Adding Palm Trees

Directions: Add the numbers on each tree. Add the top two numbers first. Then add the bottom number to the sum of the first numbers.

Sailing into Addition

Directions: What a great day to go sailing! Solve the problems on each sailboat, and you will go far!

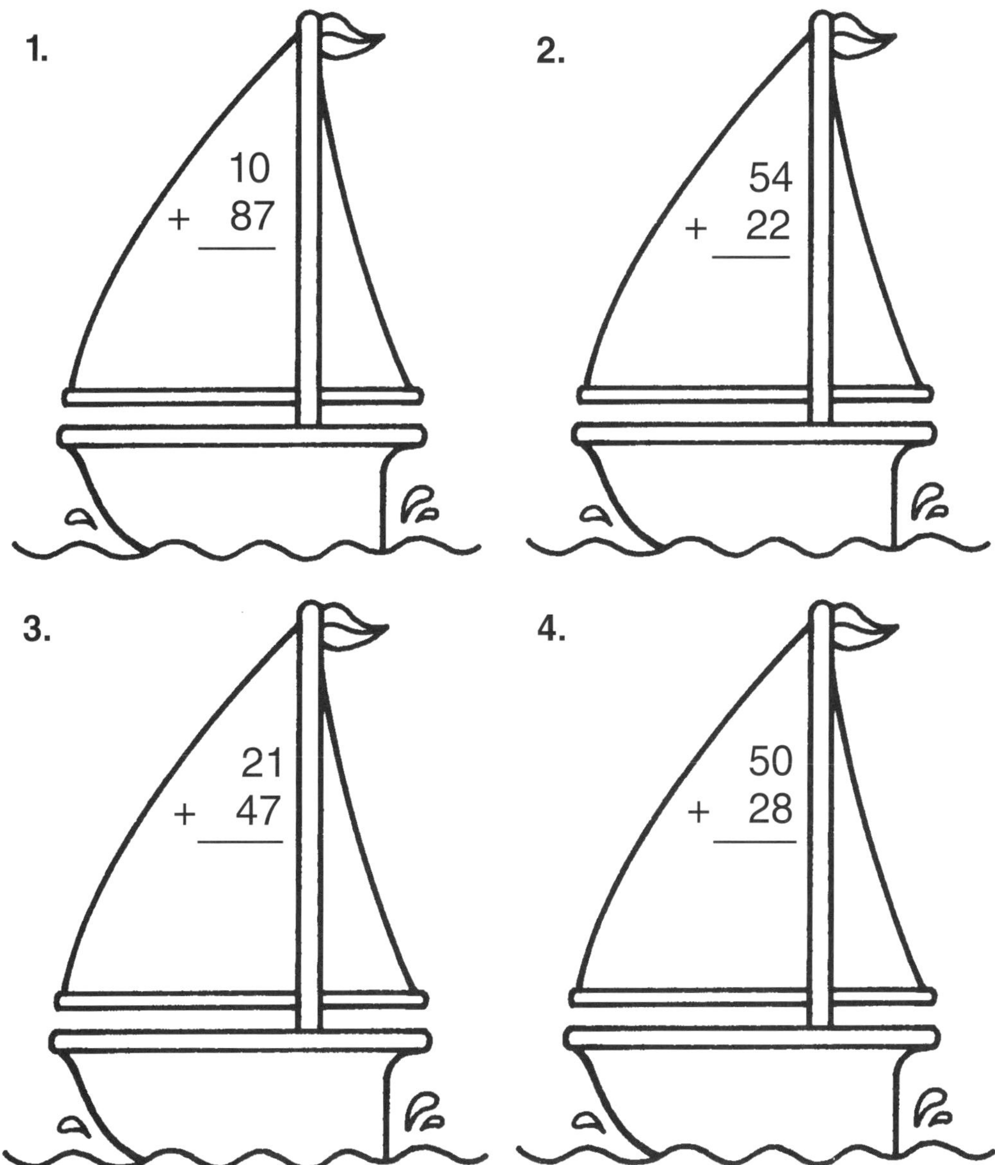

Subtraction Garden

Directions: Solve each problem. Color each flower according to the color code.

0 = pink	3 = orange
1 = blue	4 = yellow
2 = red	

1.
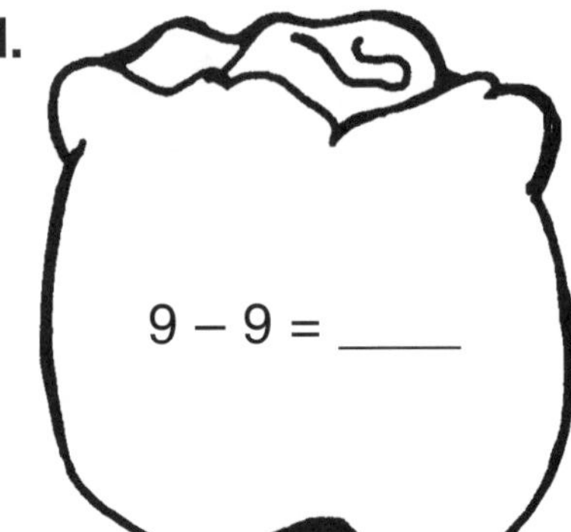

2.
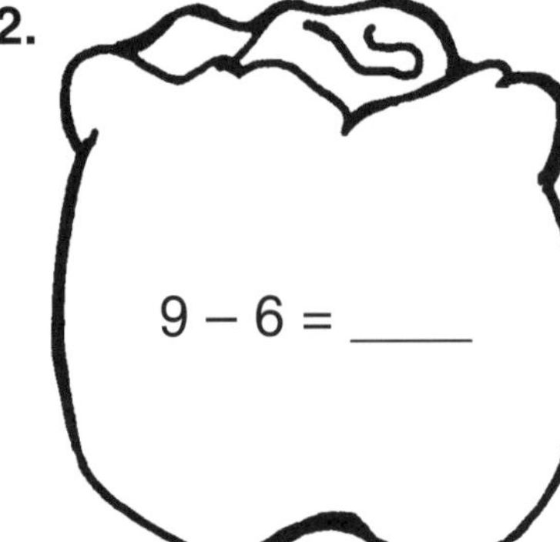

3.
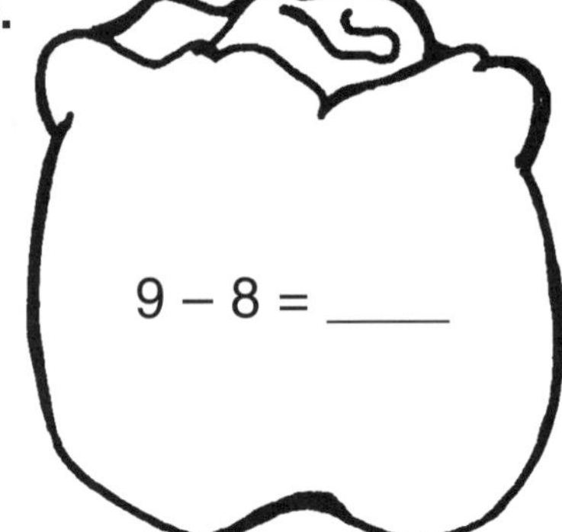

4.
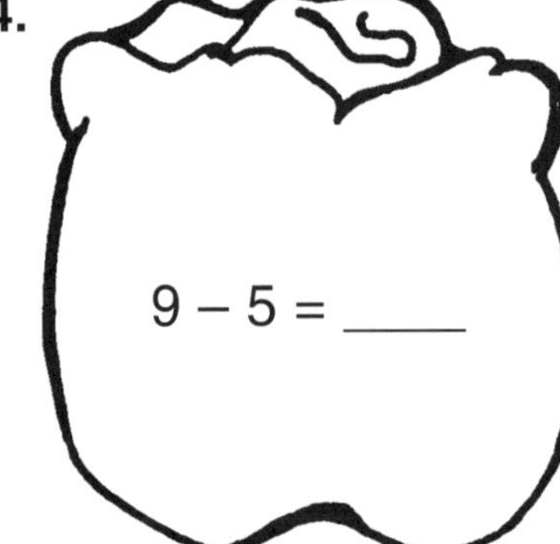

5.
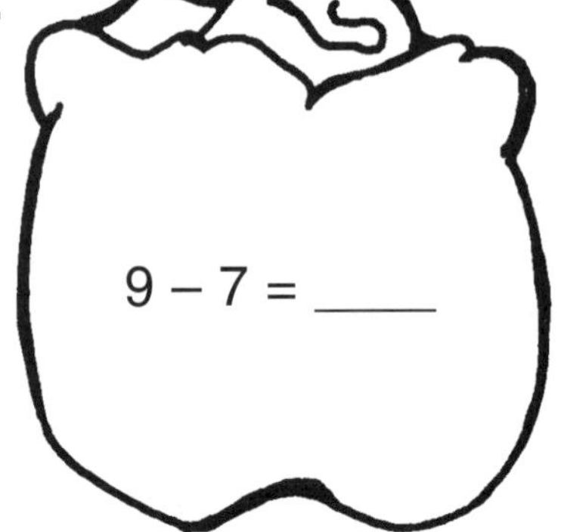

Dog Bones!

Directions: Draw a line to match each equation to its answer.

9 − 2 = _____

7 − 4 = _____

10 − 9 = _____

6 − 6 = _____

3 − 1 = _____

Through the Rain Forest

Directions: Solve each subtraction problem along the rain forest path. How fast can you get to the end?

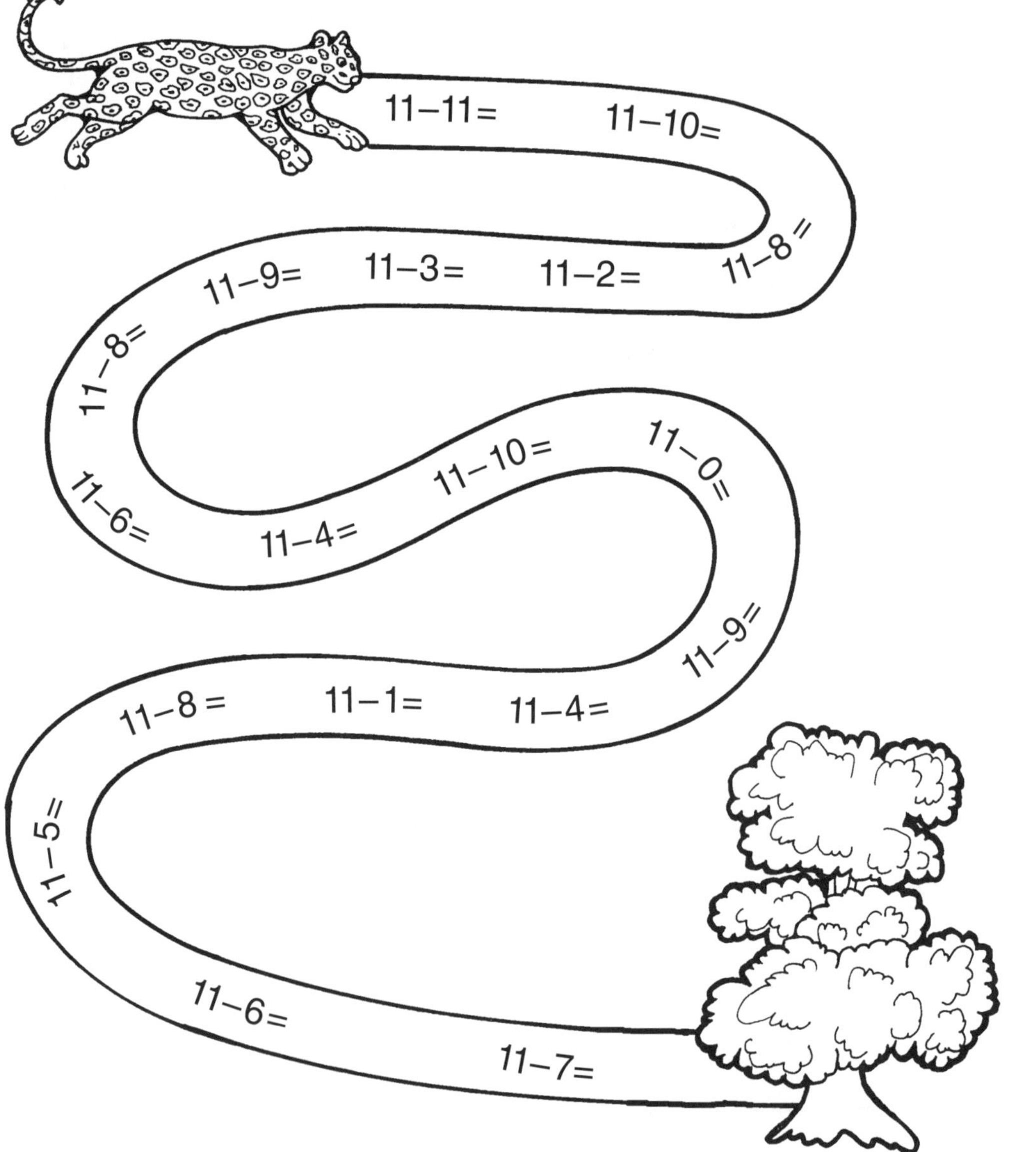

Finish Line

Directions: Color the cars. Then, write the color of the car to show the place in which each will finish the race.

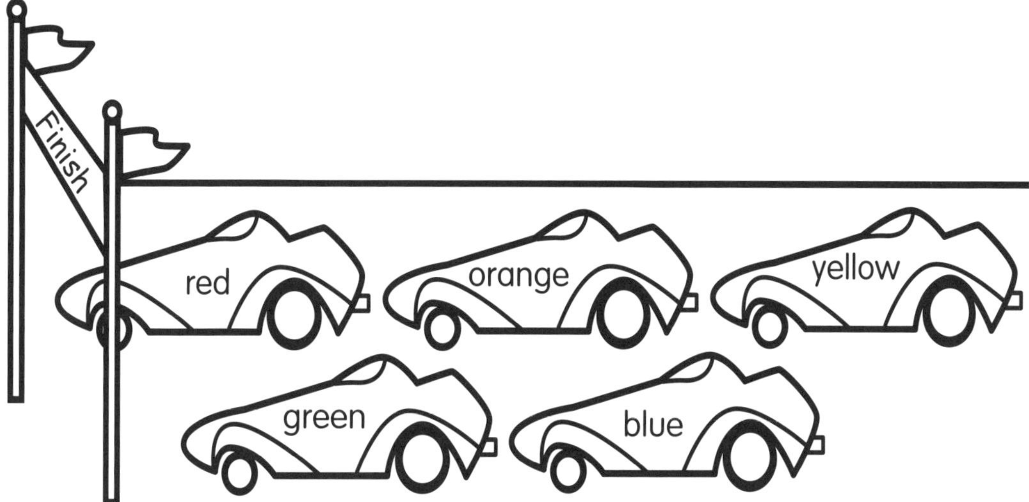

1. First   __________

4. Second   __________

2. Third   __________

5. Last   __________

3. Fourth   __________

6. What color is the car before the green car? __________

7. What color is the car after the blue car? __________

More or Less?

Directions: Write the numerals that show the number of things in each group. Color the group which is more in each row.

< is the symbol for "less than"

> is the symbol for "greater than"

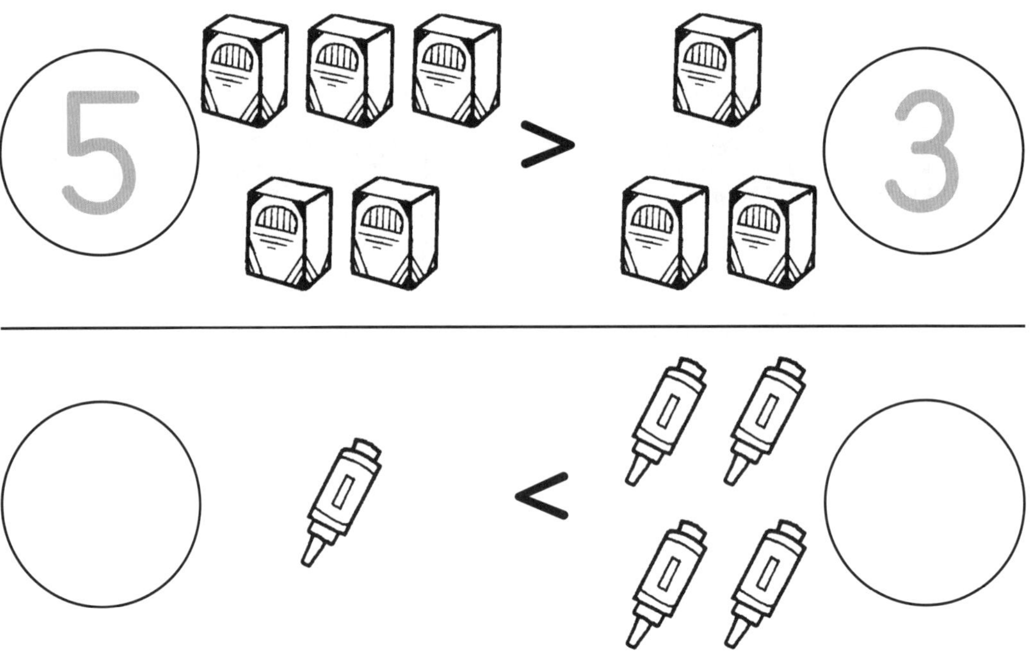

Directions: Write the correct "less than" (<) or "greater than" (>) symbol between the two numbers.

10 ◯ 8   2 ◯ 0   35 ◯ 14

64 ◯ 51   9 ◯ 11   79 ◯ 97

Pay For It

Directions: Color in the coins that could be used to pay for each item. (There may be more than one combination of coins that will work.)

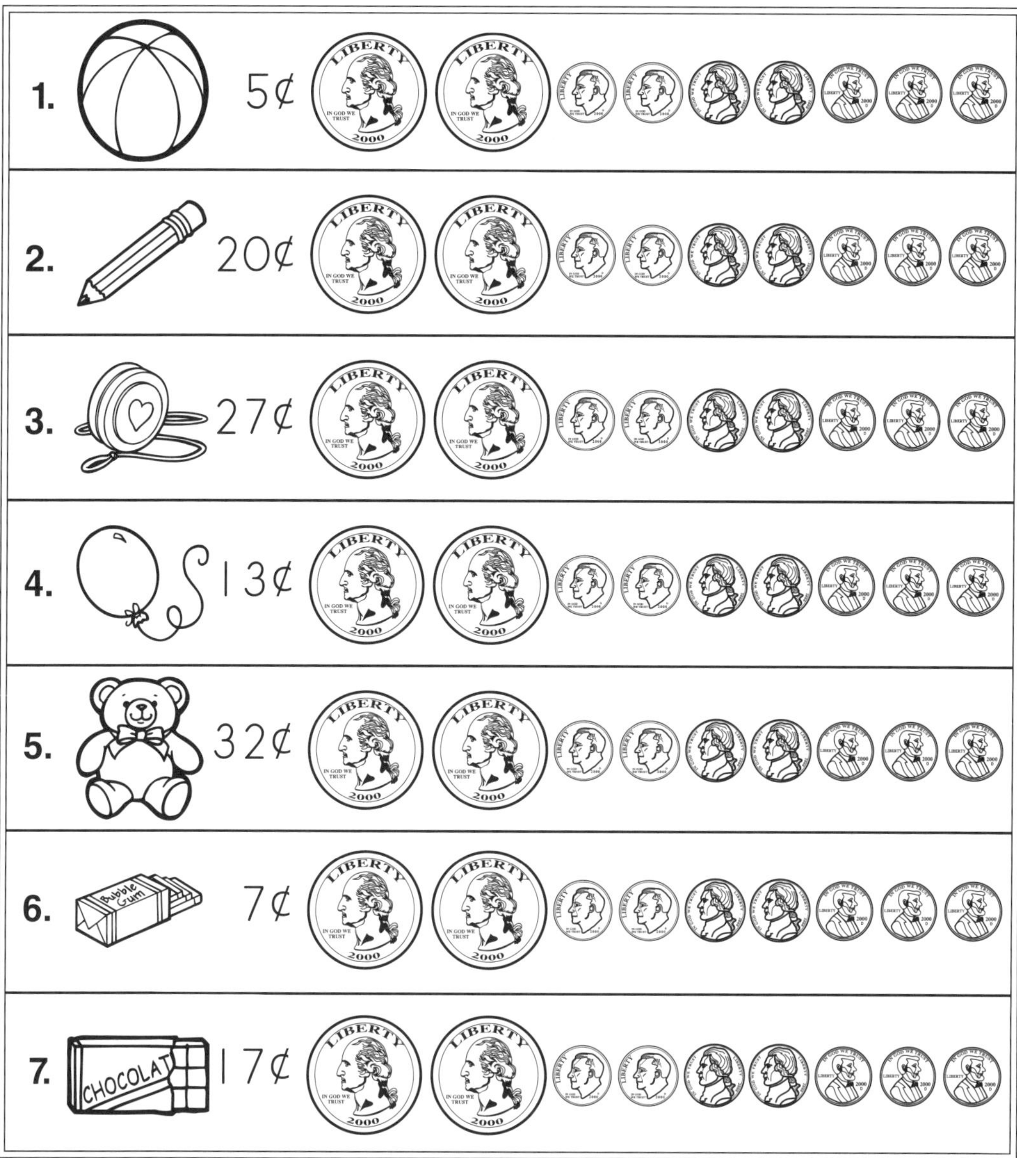

Word Problems

Directions: Read each word problem. In the box, write the answer to the question.

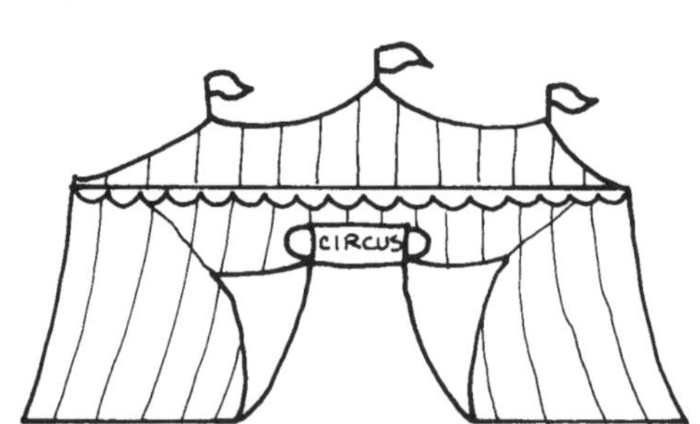

At the circus, Kenny saw 16 tigers, 14 horses, and 22 monkeys. How many animals did he see in all?

When Sandra went to the tidepools, she counted 28 starfish, 32 fish, and 46 shells. How many things did she see in all?

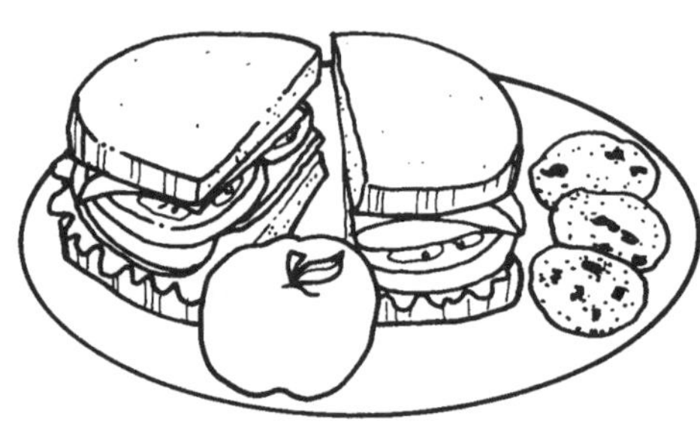

During one month, Jared ate 27 sandwiches, 23 apples, and 52 cookies. How many things did he eat in all?

Emily did 19 addition problems and 33 subtraction problems at school. At home, her mother gave her 21 more. How many problems did she solve in all?

Fish Bowl

Directions: Tally the objects in the fish bowl. Then, create a bar graph of the tallied information. The first one is done for you.

Item	Tally Marks
	I

Item	1	2	3	4	5	6	7	8

Days of the Week

Directions: Write the day that falls between the two days given.

1. Sunday   _______________   Tuesday

2. Thursday   _______________   Saturday

3. Monday   _______________   Wednesday

4. Friday   _______________   Sunday

5. Wednesday   _______________   Friday

6. Tuesday   _______________   Thursday

7. Saturday   _______________   Monday

Months of the Year

Directions: Write the month that falls between the two months given.

1. January   _______________ March

2. June   _______________ August

3. October   _______________ December

4. February   _______________ April

5. July   _______________ September

6. September   _______________ November

7. March   _______________ May

8. August   _______________ October

9. April   _______________ June

10. November   _______________ January

11. May   _______________ July

12. December   _______________ February

Best Friends

Directions: Read the story below. Answer the questions at the bottom of the page. Use complete sentences.

Best Friends

Martha and Janis are best friends. Every afternoon, the girls do their homework together. They munch on their favorite snack, popcorn. After they finish their homework, Martha and Janis go to the park. Martha takes her skates. Janis brings her scooter. They enjoy going to the park. It is good to have a best friend.

---

1. Who are the best friends? ___________________________

   ____

2. What do the girls do in the afternoon? ______________

   ____

3. Where do the girls go when they are done with their

   homework?____

   ____

Penguins

Directions: Read the passage below. Answer the questions at the bottom of the page by filling in the correct bubble.

Penguins

Penguins are unusual birds. They have feathers, but they cannot fly. They are very good at swimming. In fact, penguins spend most of their time swimming. The water is where penguins find their food. They really enjoy eating fish, squid, and krill. There are not many birds like the penguin!

1. What is a penguin's body covering?

   (a) fur   (b) feathers   (c) scales

2. What are penguins good at doing?

   (a) sliding   (b) swimming   (c) walking

3. What do penguins like to eat?

   (a) fish   (b) insects   (c) plants

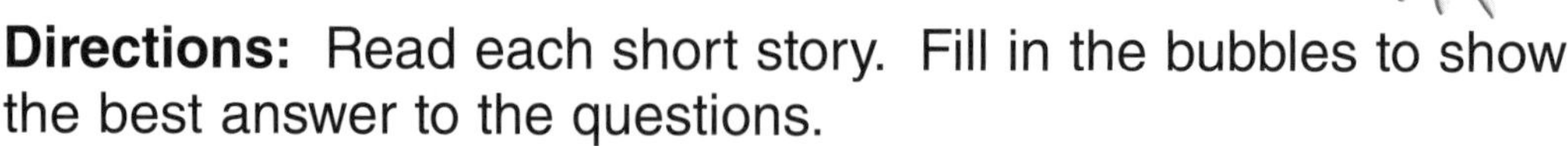

Using Inference

Directions: Read each short story. Fill in the bubbles to show the best answer to the questions.

1. Bob wears a wig. He puts on big shoes and silly clothes. Bob paints his face with make up. Then he goes to work. What is Bob's job?

   (a) fireman　　　(b) clown　　　(c) bus driver

2. Sue could hear meowing. She walked over to the tree and looked up. What was in the tree?

   (a) a bird　　　(b) a dog　　　(c) a cat

3. Mark drew a shape on his paper. He did not lift his pencil at all. The shape has no straight lines. What shape did Mark draw?

   (a) square　　　(b) circle　　　(c) triangle

4. Mary went with her mom to visit family. They visited her mom's mom. Who did Mary see?

   (a) her sister　　　(b) her uncle　　　(c) her grandma

This Award
Is Presented To

____

for

* Doing Your Best

* Trying Hard

* Not Giving Up

* Making a
  Great Effort